KNOWN YET UNKNOWN

AN ANTHOLOGY OF POEMS

COMPILED AND EDITED BY :
DR. SONIA GUPTA

DEDICATED TO

Every Woman of The World

Contents

Contents

Contents

Foreword

Known Yet Unknown : An Amazing Compilation

"You may shoot me with your words,
You may cut me with your eyes,
You may kill me with your hatefulness,
But still, like air, I'll rise."

This excerpt is from the poem "Still I Rise" by popular American poetess Maya Angelou. In these four lines, there is a complete saga of the confidence of a woman. In the modern era a woman has to live with this confidence. The description of the importance of woman can be seen in the tradition since ancient times. The Manusmriti, an important book in the Indian tradition, states that "Yatra naryastu pujyante ramante tatra Devata, yatraitaastu na pujyante sarvaastatrafalaah kriyaah", which means where women are honored, Gods reside there, and where women are dishonored, all actions fail. Presently, discussion on women is an important issue under social discussion.

When we sit down to have a meaningful conversation on an issue, first of all there are questions related to its importance and relevance. In between these two questions, a question is related to social inequality. The prevailing social inequality between men and women is not from the beginning of creation, but it is the result of different stages of social development. Ironically, the society became dynamic in the stage of social development, but the patriarchal society limited the rights of women; The result of which was that in terms of importance and authority, the social status of women kept falling day by day. Even in this zenith of development of the twenty-first century, the status of women probably still has not been as high as the Rigvedic society. After the post-Vedic period, in the Sutra period and after that in the middle ages, the continuous decline in the status of women has not been compensated till date.

In this long span of time, the life of a woman has gone through many ups and downs. Current circumstances are different. In the 21st century, changes have taken place very rapidly all over the world. There has been a change in the attitude towards women. It's a century of self-respect and confidence with challenges. In the midst of all these things, the responsibilities increase. American business executive, billionaire, and philanthropist Sheryl Kara Sandberg says very right:- "We need women at all levels, including the top, to change the dynamic, reshape the conversation, to make sure women's voices are heard and heeded, not overlooked and ignored." In an era of eroding values, it's very important to have trust in mutual relations between men and women. Every path of progress depends on the understanding of both. The noise of freedom often drowns out the real issues. We should take it seriously and positively. Women have given direction to the society in every era. They give speed to the world. In such a situation, this poem by Edna St. Vincent Millay compels a lot to think and leaves many questions:-

"I, being born a woman and distressed
By all the needs and notions of my kind,
Am urged by your propinquity to find
Your person fair, and feel a certain zest."

Literature has always emphasized the importance of existence of women. It has a long tradition in literature. Poetess Dr. Sonia Gupta's plan to bring out an anthology of various poets on these issues will definitely take this process further. She has done a special job by bringing together various poets from India and abroad in a compilation on one subject. The poems in the anthology make one feel that as an editor she understood her responsibility very well and used her capabilities to the fullest. Previously she has also proved herself as a writer & poet through various publications. Through anthology "Known Yet Unknown", various aspects of women, their existence and importance, contemporary problems and their solutions have been discussed reflecting the deep meaning of this ordinary word known as "WOMAN". A woman lives many characters in herself and proves her worth in all characters. The poets of the compilation have represented the various dimensions of female world with their full potential.

I am sure the anthology will be widely read and appreciated. Hearty congratulations and endless wishes to Dr. Sonia Gupta for editing a wonderful anthology and to all the eminent poets included in it.

Dr. Shailesh Gupta Veer
  (Poet, Reviewer, Editor)

Preface

'A woman is like a tea bag - you can't tell how strong she is until you put her in hot water'.

(Eleanor Roosevelt)

Very well said by the famous poet 'Eleanor Roosevelt' through the above quote that a WOMAN's strength cannot be fully predetermined until she is put to the test. Comparison with the tea bag is quite fitting, as it is well known that the actual strength of a tea is fully appreciated only after being subjected to hot water.

The word 'WOMAN' seems to be very small, but it beholds a deep meaning like the depth of an ocean and the vastness of the sky. The WOMAN is the angel sent by the Lord into this materialistic world and she is considered to be the architect of our society. She is God's amazing creation who is blessed with a number of virtues. Even in a WO-MAN, 'MAN' exists. She is a WOMAN only, who gives birth to a MAN. Alas! this world always underestimates her virtues, strengths, and potential and tries to suppress her identity. Yet, she remains unique. She is blessed with a golden heart that knows to love selflessly. She is an enlightening candle in the gloom of this murky world.

Since her birth, she blossoms many relations playing vivid roles like a daughter, mother, sister and partner. As a daughter, being the angel of her parents, she fills their life with joy, love, and smile. As a sister, she threads a garland of love and care. As a partner, she accompanies her soulmate in every odd and even phase of life and enlightens a candle of love in his world. As a mother, she is an embodiment of blessings, love and care for her children. In nutshell, it can be beautifully said that in every form, she is a paragon of LOVE. A WOMAN's heart is as tender as soft petals, but when the time comes, it can turn into a burning fire to destroy all the evils, sins, and crimes that try to destroy her self-respect and identity. History reveals, how she has shown her power in the form of 'DURGA', 'LAKSHMI BAI', 'SATI', and many more. Her inner strength can't be known truly.

Today, the time has changed drastically and the WOMAN of today is not considered to be docile and caged in four walls. She is touching the heights of success, wearing the wings of self-belief and determination. She is achieving more than a man. She has created miracles through her magical wand. She is like the previous Prime Ministar of India, thr late 'Indira Gandhi' and 'the present President 'Droupadi Murmu' who have shown their potential of leading this Man-predominated world through their WOMAN power. There are several such names all around. In conclusion, though the term WOMAN is known to everyone, yet the deep meaning hidden in this word is not completely known. That is what the title of this book "Known Yet Unknown" signifies. What a WOMAN can do, she herself does not know. Because she is not only a WOMAN but a paragon of abundant virtues.

I have got fifteen independent poetry books, several anthologies, and other literary contributions on vivid themes. But since long, this was one of my dreams as a WOMAN poet to gather an anthology of poems on WOMAN composed by different minds. That inspired me to take an initiative for compiling and editing this anthology. The current anthology "Known Yet Unknown ", is a collection of 50 poems dedicated to all the WOMEN. These poems have been composed by 50 poets from different countries of the world. The versatile poets have dipped their emotions into the ink of their pen, and have painted such a wonderful canvas, that represents the beauty and value of this small word that is known as 'WOMAN'. This is not only a book but a tribute and honuor to all the women of the world.

I hope, after reading these beautiful verses composed by beautiful souls, your heart will enchant the songs of WOMAN saluting her for all the virtues she has been gifted by Almighty. I believe, that through these verses, the vision of society towards WOMEN will definitely change to a positive side.

Yours sincerely
Dr. Sonia Gupta

Acknowledgements

Gratitude is a single word, but deep meaning it beholds. I usually hear these words – "If we say Thank you to someone, it means we are bowing our head in front of that Lord only". We can forget anything in life, but we should never forget to thank someone who has helped or motivated us in any way.

I am a medical professional, I never thought that one day I would become a writer, poet and author. It is all a miracle and a dream for me. But now it has become my passion, inspiration, and an integral part of my life. It's all by God's grace that he honoured me with such a unique gift.

First of all, I thank the Goddess of knowledge and wisdom *Maa Saraswati,*who gave me the strength to complete this work and encouraged me to pick up my pen to compile, edit, and prepare this anthology.

In the world, everything changes, but one thing that never ever changes is *our parents.* Heartfelt thanks to my parents for their faith and showering their infinite blessings on me. Special thanks to my father who has left this materialistic world attaining the embrace of the divine Lord. He had been my inspiration and will be forever and his teachings illuminate my life's pathway like an enlightening candle. My mother is my best friend, who has always accompanied me in every odd and even phase of life. At every step of this project, her guidance and blessings were with me. She motivated me to complete this huge task. I am blessed to have my two younger brothers who are pillars of my life. They are younger than me, but the biggest booster of inspiration, who encouraged me to accomplish even the impossible tasks in my life. A token of thanks to my dear brothers.

Huge bundle of gratitude to all the authors and poets, who have put their endless efforts by contributing their wonderful poems signifying the theme of this anthology. Most of the poets are much senior to me and I pay my regard and honour to all of them for their full cooperation from the day one of this project till the last moment, respecting my guidelines and instructions. Each poem is filled with vivid colours of emotions, respect, love, appreciation, and honour toward femineity which has painted a beautiful canvas that would be worthwhile to preserve forever in the hearts of readers. Without all of you, this collection would not have been possible. Once again, my heartfelt thanks to all of you for your love, support, and encouragement.

My words are not enough to thank *Dr. Shailesh Veer Gupta* sir, for writing a wonderful foreword for this anthology. Without his support and blessings, this anthology was not possible. He not only reviewed these poems but also guided me at every step in completing this project. He is not only a good writer but a humble personality who always encourages other writers. A heartful thanks to you dear sir.

Teachers are the selfless builders of our life, A word of thanks to all respected teachers who always showed me the right path in my life and brimmed my heart with their blessings.

Friends are the precious ornaments gifted by God, who without any blood relation, make a bonding of forever relation. My regards and love to all friends far and near.

Last but not least, it will be unfair if I forget to thank the *Notion Press publication* through which this book is going to be published. Thanks to entire team for the cooperation.

Thank you, readers, fellow poets, and friends for all your love and appreciation!!!

Dr. Sonia Gupta

Know About The Editor

Dr. Sonia Gupta (Mohali, Punjab, India)

Dr. Sonia Gupta is a writer, poetess, reviewer, editor and translator. She writes in English, Hindi, and Punjabi languages. By profession she is a Dentist (MDS) with major specialization in Oral and Maxillofacial Pathology. Poetry is her passion. She has established herself as a renowned author after getting her Fifteen independent books published till date, out of which Five are in Hindi and Ten are in English language. Her English books are poetic collections entitled 'Spectrum of Life', 'Canvas of Life..With My Pen', 'Fountain of Inspirations', 'Meeting My Soulmate', 'Silent Verses',

'Mysterious Musings of Life', 'Agony of Life', 'Miracle of Virtues', 'Acrostic Motivations', and 'There is No Darkness'. Her first English novel is coming soon. Her Hindi books include Four collections of poetry entitled 'Zindagi Gulzar Hai', 'Ummid Ka Diya', 'Kabhi Jalte Kabhi Bujhte Chirag'and 'Kuch Ankahe Ehsas'. One of her books of stories 'Aadmi Bne Rehne Ka Dhong' has been published recently.

She writes in vivid genera of English literature like poetry, stories, essays, letters, songs and many more. She is an active member of various poetry groups on Facebook and has won several awards in writing competitions organized by those groups and other literary platforms. She won a Gold and Silver Medal in a Poetic world Cup contest held by Nigeria in Feb and May 2018 respectively, PRASANNA JENN MEMORIAL AWARD -2018 by the Asian Literary Society, and 5th rank in the International Essay writing competition on 'Skin complexion discrimination' organized by literary society, India in March 2018. One of her essays 'Our role & responsibilities toward nation was selected in a National essay writing competition and is a part of the book 'Youth as Nation Builders; a collection of 41 essays published by Lab Academia.

Her literary journey continues with a great endeavour. Her writings reflect her closeness and deep love for nature, life, spirituality and humanity. For her, poetry is a God-gifted boon and she wishes to fly high wearing the wings of poetry. She has contributed to more than 100 National and International English anthologies so far. She is a regular contributor to various National and International magazines, newspapers and journals. She has translated many poems by other poets from different regions of the world into English, Hindi and Punjabi languages. She runs a blog about the Punjabi translation of English poems by different poets throughout the world.

She is a famous name in Hindi literature also. She writes stories, essays, letters, articles, and vivid genera of Hindi poetry. Besides her independent Hindi books, her Hindi writings are part of several International and National anthologies, newspapers and magazines. She has won many awards for her Hindi writings. Her first poetry book in the Punjabi language is coming soon. Her many projects are underway.

Besides poetry, she is fond of painting, singing, cooking, knitting, designing, stitching and embroidery. She has won many awards in Art competitions. Many of her paintings have been placed on the cover pages of various anthologies. Even she has designed the cover pages of her two English anthologies entitled "Fountain of Inspirations" and "Canvas of Life..With My Pen". She is actively contributing to the literature via her literary YouTube channel, Facebook page, Blog and Instagram page.

Dr. Sonia has gone through many ups and downs in her life that directed her vision toward suffering and she expresses that with her pen. She considers her parents her biggest inspiration, who have always motivated her in each and every phase of her life. She lost her father in 2019, who was an English professor. She is living her life following his teachings and footprints. She has got two younger brothers, and she considers them the pillars of her life.

Dr. Sonia Gupta is a renowned name in her professional field also. She is working as an Associate Professor in the Oral Pathology Dept. at a Dental College in Mohali. She serves the community as a doctor by providing dental care. She has 25 scientific publications in PubMed and Scopus indexed National and International Journals with the first authorship and many more are under review. She is also working on three textbooks on her subject of specialization. She is acting as a reviewer of various Medical and Dental Journals. She actively takes part in various conferences, workshops, community health programs, and events and has presented several research papers and posters. She is a dedicated academician with a mission of making her students excel in their subjects and in developing their multitalented skills.

CONTACT DETAILS

- **ADDRESS-** #95/3, Adarsh Nagar, Dera Bassi, Dist: Mohali, Punjab-140507, India.
- **MOBILE-** 6280420736
- **FACEBOOK ID** - 100004964983747@facebook.com
- **FACEBOOK PAGE** - https://www.facebook.com/sonia4840/
- **BLOG** - http://drsoniablogspot.blogspot.in/
- **PUNJABI TRANSLATION BLOG** - https://www.blogger.com/blog/settings/
6938540478443911129hl=en#:~:text=passionatepunjabijourney.blogspot.com
- **E MAIL** - drsoniagupta82@gmail.com
- **YOUTUBE CHANNEL** - https://www.youtube.com/channel/UCKF2jM5P8VDjZ9fBZLBTRHA
- **INSTAGRAM ID-** https://instagram.com/gdrsonia?igshid=YmMyMTA2M2Y=

Known Yet Unknown

O' she seems to be a silently flowing river,
But a deep ocean she is actually,
She beholds a heart as tender as the petals of a flower,
But dwells abundant power deeply.

She spreads smiles to the entire world,
But an oasis of tears resides within her,
She is considered to be home's bird,
But the whole universe, she can conquer.

She is given the titles of daughter, sister, mother and wife,
But in the true sense, she is a leader leading this world,
She is treated as a slave of man's pride,
But she is the queen of queens in real words.

She is called by a little word,
But she is a complete book actually,
'Known yet unknown' to this world,
None can understand her fully.

© **Dr. Sonia Gupta**

An Intro About The Reviewer

Dr. Shailesh Gupta Veer (Fatehpur, UP, India)

He is a poet, critic and multi-prize winner. His literary works are characterized with a high degree of creativity and aunthencity. He is a bilingual, writes in English & Hindi both. He is a blogger, where he regulars posts his poems. He is admin and moderator of various poetry groups on Facebook. He has edited about two dozen literary books and several magazines time to time. His poetry has been published in various literary magazines, journals, anthologies and websites. He has won many awards in the field of poetry and literature. His poems have been translated into Chinese, Greek, German, French, Azerbaijani, Arabic, Italian, Serbian, Croatian, Portuguese, Nepali, Punjabi & some other languages. He is the editor of Micro poetry Cosmos and the associate editor of The Voice of Creative Research. He is also a reviewer and promoter of poetry and literature. His poetry attracts hearts of many, while forcing brains to get calculative. His love for human values, nature, philosophy and the spiritual world is insurmountable. All these can clearly be seen in his works of poetry. He was declared a Literary Icon in December 2018 by TV program You and Literature Today from Nigeria. His poems were read on The Dear John Show of Warrington, England. He is PhD in Archaeology. He is an inspiration for the budding writers.

- Dr. Shailesh Gupta Veer

    (Poet, Reviewer, Editor)

- Address: 18/17, Radha Nagar, Fatehpur, UP, India , Pin : 212601
- Mobile : 9839942005
- Email : editorsgveer@gmail.com

A Big Salute

She bears
dual responsibilities
on her shoulders,
and always
brings happiness.

Despite the grief and pain,
Despite being neglected,
Smile on her face
Never fades.

A woman is always
A working woman.
A big salute.

© **Dr. Shailesh Gupta Veer**

List Of Poets

(Paperback, 1ˢᵗ Edition, @ January 2023)

Compiled & Edited By: Dr. Sonia Gupta

1. These Broken Lines

These broken lines,
Yet curved at corners,
Not only narrate my story of life,
But also talk about my path.

Those above and below my eyes,
Creating an abyss for them to rest,
With dense silence,
Trying to hide in my broken smiles.

I don't regret, and am proud of these broken uneven lines,
At least these are honest,
May play hide and seek with numerals,
But don't cheat, they are...the one's Survivors.

From the tempest of being a WOMAN,
A struggler, a warrior, a triumphant,
Yes, I AM A WOMAN,
I am proud of being a WOMAN.

© Aarti Mittal

Aarti Mittal (Mumbai, Maharashtra, India)

aarti.amittal@gmail.com

She is a bilingual poet. She writes short skits with morals for children. She follows the religion of humanity, compassion and love and tries to spread the same. She believes that her writings can win hearts and help to bring some change to make this world a better place. Her writings also include themes based on women's empowerment and child exploitation. She is a teacher by profession.

2. Potential Me

I am a woman,
A Durga devi in disguise,
The gentle push of a lioness,
Leads the pride, consoles the cries.

I am a woman,
Full of compassion,
Abound with confidence,
Brimming with fashion.

I am a woman,
Don't you judge my potential power's capabilities,
Let it loose,
And you will be shaken when you recognize the possibilities.

I am a woman,
Keeping the order of my thousand goals,
Loving my body,
And loving my soul.

© Aditi Karthick

Aditi Karthick (Chennai, Tamil Nādu, India)

vmpselvi@gmail.com

She is a 13-year-old young writer who wrote her first poem 'I love you Mom' when she was in Kindergarten and won first prize at the Minnesota State Fair. She loves reading and writing poems and stories. She is also fond of creating digital illustrations. She wishes to fly high wearing the wings of poetry.

3. A Woman of Virtues

I am a woman,
God's indescribable gift,
My unique abilities are a blessing to the world,
Gentleness and softness are my words.

I am a woman, of inestimable value,
A great queen, of unfathomable virtue,
Breed to nurture and to train,
Come to complete and not to compete.

I am a woman, more precious than silver,
Made to love, a cheerful giver,
Created to help, a problem solver,
Born to guide, a thoughtful spender.

A tender mother, and pensive manager I am,
Not because I give birth,
But because I give care,
The world can attest, to a woman of virtues I am.

© Ajayi Oluwasegun Samson

Ajayi oluwsegun Samson (Osogtbo, Osun, Nigeria)

ajayiolusegun49@gmail.com

He is a poet and a creative writer. Poetry is his passion. He writes poems, essays and stories from his Secondary School. He has won several prizes and awards during his schooling at both National and Local levels, in debate competitions and essay writing. He is an active member of several poetry groups on Facebook. Presently, he is pursuing nursing.

4. Not Enough

When you think…
You are not enough,
Keep your gaiety, your cadence,
Keep your informal elegance,
And your eccentricities,
Keep your clumsy twirls for,
A bit of winsomeness.
Cherish your mediocrities.

For they charm like rustic wines,
Do not polish to perfection,
Your endearing waywardness,
Keep your old laces and lipsticks,
Blue brooches and bright spangles,
The ones that smile at you,
Celebrate your frivolities,
Drift the disapprovals aside,
And marvel at the wondrous you.

© Dr. Balesh Jindal

Dr. Balesh Jindal (Delhi, India)

jindalbalesh@yahoo.co.in

She is a renowned artist with a creative portfolio of art, poetry and photographs. She has published three poetry books; a coffee table book 'A Hundred Dreams', 'Dear Father' and 'The Reluctant Doctor a Memoir'. She is a physician by profession; a graduate of the prestigious Lady Hardinge Medical College in Delhi and has had a professional medical practice for the last forty years. She has received several awards in her professional and literary fields.

5. Love Tiff

The ground focus dimmed a difference
That was a fairy tale, adopted
This has been a tanned one
The former was born out of shape
The latter gave vent to the worldly.

The throb of a maiden date killed
Many moments of tussle yielded
The fruit of ripe joy, had dinner
Dropped her to mom's lodge
Basted the edifice of dream I hatched.

On point to the fairy tale forlorn
In between the lines
The tug of emotion got killed us
The outside faded the bubbly charm
The inside got atrophied.

© **Basudev Paul**

Basudev Paul (Malbazar, West Bengal, India)

basudevpaul01@gmail.com

He is a poet, writer and author. His poetry is a psalm; a sacred song of his life felt at the gloaming of his career. His poetical composition aiming at the worship of God chants as a canticle for humanity. He has published one English poetry book; "The Permanent Transient". He is M.A. in English, and has worked as a teacher with thirty-seven years of teaching experience.

6. I Mean It

Why does my spirit make a nose dive?
Why should someone try to degrade me?
I have every right to make myself happy,
Engrossed in my writing world of creativity.

Am I destined to waste this life?
Only doing the chores heaped on me,
Just because I am a wife?
Don't I have my own life?

Am I not entitled to free time?
To spend it on me,
In pursuit of my hobby?
Thinking about my happiness only?

I am I a small I, still, I am I,
And I mean it so,
No one is my Lord,
And I mean it, really.

©Bharati Nayak

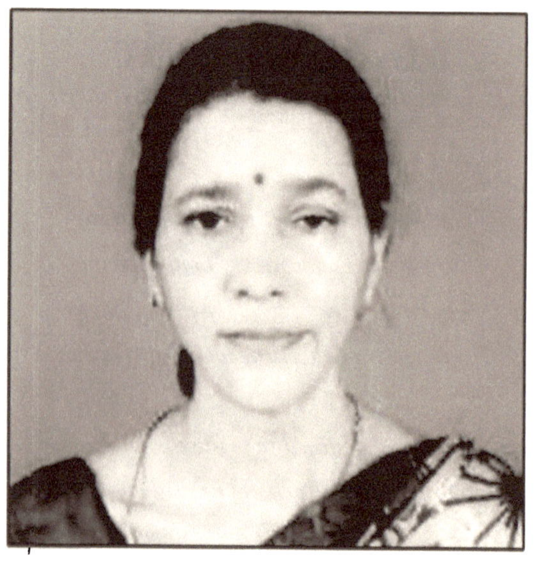

Bharati Nayak *(Bhubaneswar, Odisha, India)*

bharati1962@rediffmail.com

She is a bilingual poet, writer, translator and editor. She has so far published two Odia poetry collections, one book of translation of South African poetess Adiela Akkoo's book 'Lost in A Quatrain' into Odia, two English poetry collections as sole author and six books as co-author with other poets. She is a postgraduate in Political Science.

7. Stop This Discrimination

I am a strong pillar of the nation's strength,
Given the chance can cover any length,
I bear all misdemeanors with full patience,
Put to grueling tests of human endurance,

I am used as a doormat or window curtain,
You sell and buy me in dowry bargain,
We are no commodities but living beings,
Why stifle our dreams and our feelings.

Give me enough rope to widen our space,
Don't violate my right, don't transgress,
No more harassment no intimidation,
Times have changed no discrimination.

O, Let me live a life solely of my own,
Fly free like birds in the high spatial zone,
Draw no lines le'me seek my own horizons,
Life beyond fore walls no veiled seclusion.

©Birendu Kumar Sinha

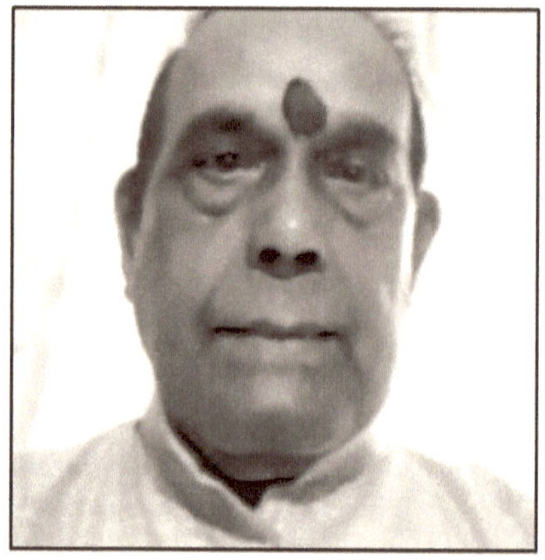

Birendu Kumar Sinha (Patna, Bihar, India)

birenduksinha14@gmail.com

He is a Freelance journalist, short story writer and poet. He has authored two poetry books namely 'Fragrance of earth' and 'Symphony of love'. He is an active member of various poetic forms on Facebook. He has won several awards for his poems. He served as a English lecturer and Senior Management Officer at State Bank of India.

8. Not Mine

That city I left was not mine,
When I stepped into its long gateway,
I didn't get fragrance in flowers,
That garden was not mine.

The city's tall edifices, its narrow alleys,
The screams floated from its rooms,
Loaded heavy stones over tiny hearts,
Those rooms were not mine.

When I got drenched in rapt In the sticky rains,
When the splashes enmeshed around,
That odd time rain had not come for me,
That rain was not mine.

The city's lanes, the rose petals, the smiles of peacocks,
Flowers fitted in my bosom's folds,
While walking there, the fragrance of existence touched my heart,
Despite why that existence was not mine.

© Boby Borah

Boby Borah (Tinsukia, Assam, India)

bobyborah30@gmail.com

She is a poet and author. She has authored 3 books and edited several magazines. Her poems and articles are published in several newspapers in Assam. She has been awarded several awards in her professional and literary journey. She is M.A. in literature, Founder/Principal of Shankardev Shishu Niketan school. She is also the president of Doom Dooma Mahila Samiti and secretary of Sundoram Kobi Sanmilan.

9. Shadows

Oh man,
Why you take so much pleasure to kill?
Is this a conspiracy of your life?
A greater betrayal of my affection.

My life here is always under threat
In some way or the other
Killing has become a habit
The air carries the odour of crime
We are all nothing but shadows
To your insane mind.

All are afraid of death
To their egoistic minds
Nothing is original here
Which one you call your own?
Shoot me if that's your wish
Death cannot snatch away
What I have not obtained From life.

© B.S. Saroja

B. S. Saroja (Bangalore, Karnataka, India)

bssaroja1953@gmail.com

She is a poet, writer and author. Her poems and writes have been published in many anthologies, magazines, and periodicals. Poetry is her lifelong passion. She is also a social worker. She is a postgraduate in Kannada and a graduate in Science and a Diploma holder in Commerce and is retired as a personal secretary to the Managing Director of a business organization.

10. You May Think

You may think...
I am an ordinary woman,
What do you think that I am not,
I can do whatever you can't imagine,
I have climbed the Everest,
Have crossed the English Channel,
What do you want more?

You may think...
I should be in the kitchen,
Yes I would be there for a few moments,
There also I would prepare the tastiest cuisine,
Some may think I am an entertaining tool,
That you never think from now on,
The greatest decision I make for the generation,
I am Droupadi Murmu inspiring billions,
Think not I am an ordinary human...

© Damodar Boruah

Damodar Boruah (Dergaon, Assam, India)

damodarboruah14@gmail.com

He is a multi-award-winning poet, writer and translator at the National and International levels. He has composed more than five hundred poems to date. He is an active member of various poetry groups on social media. His recent book 'From A Father to A Daughter...to touch the sky!' has become a great hit. His motto: 'Create Farmers, Create Entrepreneurs, Create Markets, Create Stories.' is widely accepted among many stakeholders. By profession, he is a Small Tea Grower and farmer.

11. Puzzle

My desires duly suppressed,
and consoled,
in the elemental longing,
absorbed and lost,
silently within,
I do cry.

Peering into the paling sky,
I find myself,
Imprisoned,
as a lonely moon,
in the vast,
but vacant sky.

©Dasharath Naik

Dasharath Naik (Sundargarh, Odisha, India)

dasharath23664@gmail.com

He is a poet, writer and editor. Poetry is his passion and he writes for pleasure. His main motto is to spread peace, love, and humanity through his poetry. He is the Admin of various poetry groups on Facebook. He has contributed to several anthologies, magazines and journals, both Nationally and Internationally. Currently, he is working as a Reader(SS) in English.

12. Woman- A Blessing

I am a woman...
A highly dignified creature,
The mother of this universe,
Without whom, this world would become blind.

I am a woman...
The eternal source of humanity,
Through whom the words, 'pity, sympathy and compassion',
Seem precious and important.

I am a woman...
The kindest nature's boon,
I always try to glorify my family,
Sacrificing my dreams and career.

I am a woman...
Whom God had given extra-terrestrial powers,
To give birth to a child,
Thus, I am happy bearing a life inside me.

©Debashrita Basu

Debashrita Basu (Kolkata, West Bengal, India)

debashritaroy14@gmail.com

She is a passionate lover of nature. She loves to travel and her hobby is writing poems through exploring things around her and by widening her observations. She is a member of various poetry groups on Facebook. She has won several awards in literature. She is an M.A. degree holder and an English teacher by profession.

13. There Is Always More

Being a woman you're assigned to multi-tasked roles,
More or less life has offered.

It's all about how much you're packed,
And how you're going to deliver.

Don't mind being singled out while missing the herd,
You're certainly going to get back that pace.

Firmly by keeping with that flow,
It's a privilege to stand alone.

Being indifferent toward your highs and lows,
Tough, rough patches of life's conundrums are so genuine.

No matter how life goes,
There is always more to you.

© Diptirekhu Das

Diptirekha Das (Bhubaneswar, Odisha, India)

diptirekhadas73@gmail.com

She is a bilingual poet and also a blogger. She has a strong passion for literature. She has contributed to many National & International anthologies. Her articles related to women's empowerment have been published in several social forums. She is a post-graduate in Economics.

14. Let Me Introduce Myself

I am a woman,
I've many subtitles,
Infinite professions I pursue,
Soft, sober and caring mother.

Precision in the name of operating scissors, bandages,
Arguments to seek justice, truth,
Soar in the air with a broad and right vision,
Wandering to realize the ultimate, portraying mercy.

Sometimes seductive, sometimes saint,
Many veils on a single face,
Called to be a woman,
Supposed to be kind, pure, and innocent.

But it can take any mould,
To be timid or else bold,,
I love to eavesdrop, gossip
Paint, polish, however, educated yet have to undergo 'Labour'.

© Gargi Saha

Gargi Saha (Varanasi, Uttar Pradesh, India)

gargi.paik@gmail.com

She is a creative writer since her childhood. She has published two poetry books namely 'The Muse in My Salad Days' and 'Letters to Him'. Recently she received the Rabindranath Tagore Memorial Award and the Independence Day Award for poetry. She is a member of various poetry groups on Facebook. She is M.A and M.Phil. in English. Presently she edits scientific research papers.

15. She as I am

She is a sea of wild waves,
But if you look deeply,
You can find a deep ocean of...
Crystal clear waters and serenity,
She can be a devastating hurricane.

However, she often overflows sweetness,
She is like an indomitable colt,
But most of the time, her heart,
melts into delicacies of love.

She can be anything she wants, because...
Redemption comes through her gestures, actions...verses...
Into her she is an untouchable sanctuary, living harmoniously,
With her veiled passion, smooth wise, generous heart...
Granted and shared in perfect discretion...
This same life exploding into her chest challenges her...

Expands in wonders of multiple options simply for being a woman...

© *Gelda Castro Tello*

Gelda Castro Tello(Reo de Janerio, Brazil)

gel2015c@gmail.com

She is a poet, writer and artist. She started writing poetry in English, actively participating in several literary groups, and many anthologies and has been participating in many English Poetic Festivals. She has written more than a thousand poems. Poetry is her motto as an antidote to the ills of the world. She graduated in Portuguese-English languages.

16. Womb Her Temple

Quiz contest question
Define God in one word
"Mom" won first prize
Mom is not just a woman
She is God's female version
Descended on earth with a mission

Mom equals God
Many temples exist for God
Why none for Mom?
Divine voice whispered
God's temples have lifeless statues
"Womb" is Mom's temple with a live foetus

© Dr Hitendra Mehta

Dr. Hitendra Mehta (Mumbai, Maharashtra, India)

hitendramehta@rediffmail.com

He is an IIM L Alumnus and a Polymath- poet, artist, social activist and socio-economic thinker, He was a semi-finalist in International Poetry Contest, and Silver Medallist in the All India Drawing Competition. He has authored two books. He is a member of the World Human Rights Protection, Commission, a volunteer at the UN Online Volunteer Program, and featured in Gujarati Midday and Tata Sky interview.

17. The Custodian of Spring

At the onset of each new sprouting Springtime,
You will hear her sweet voice happily trill,
Over hillsides, fields, farms, flower-pots full.
Imbued with bright promise bursting, exuberant.

Spritely champion, sylph-lithe … evergreen,
Skin mottled ivory-lemon, virescent green,
Camouflage of the forest, trees, and leaves,
Hair of lustrous grasses, plaited-woven wild florals.

Eyes the verdurous depth of ephemeral aurora dreams,
Singing songs to germinate sentient embryonic sleep,
Not a single seed falls by nature's wayside season,
Spring blesses each and everyone with life's potential.

Green-fingered is she, naturally vegetative, healthful,
Propagation, aliveness, birth, responds to her siren call,
Dynamic beginnings of all, growing strong and tall,
The Custodian of Spring –Woman - gives life to all.

© Janet Stoyel

Janet Stoyel MBE (Taunton, Somerset, UK)

j.stoyel@btinternet.com

She writes poems as her passion. She is an active member of various poetry groups on Facebook and has won several awards in poetic contests. She is a Master of Philosophy, UCE Batchelor of Arts (Hons); a Winston Churchill Fellow; Queen Elizabeth Scholar, Wingate Scholar, and Holder of: the AILU Lifetime Award. She was presented with an MBE from Queen Elizabeth II, for services to Photonics, Textiles, Art and Design.

18. When a Woman Bleeds

When a woman bleeds,
In rhythm with the moon,
The cycle of fertility she feeds,
Nature's promise to attune.

A channel is she to those,
Souls looking for a rebirth,
Her menstrual flows,
Are as the life-sustaining rivers of the earth.

She who could hold her sword pure,
And her blood in battle sacrifice,
Why then is her blood unpure
If shed through an orifice?

No impurity this, no taboo,
A woman's bleeding is just fine,
Like rain, sun and harvest too,
This is a cycle divine.

© *Kamar Sultana Sheik*

Kamar Sultana Sheik (Bangalore, Karnataka, India)

sultana_sheik@yahoo.co.in

She is a poet, writing mostly on themes of spirituality, mysticism and nature with a focus on Sufi Poetry. She has contributed to various anthologies and won several prizes. Her most recent publication,' The Golden Dawn' (A Covid Times release) won the Poet of the year award 2020 from Galaxy Foundation. She creates artwork to create environmental awareness. A blogger and content writer, Sultana calls herself a wordsmith. She is a post-graduate in Botany and worked in her professional career spanning 18 years.

19. Today's Woman

The woman of today,
Is not just docile anyway.

Her uniqueness is her versatility,
Anybody need not feel of her as a charity.

She is ok with sharing responsibility,
Ready to face any odds and evens in life boldly.

She is not only a woman,
She is the earth in the face of humans.

She is the creator of nature,
Daughter, mother , and a sister.

Rolls She plays the best,
In her has the power of zest.

It is everybody's duty,
To make sure her status remains of a deity.

© *Kavita Sangras Kanherikar*

Kavita Sangras Kanherikar

(Hyderabad, Telangana, India)
kavi.sangras@gmail.com

She is a trilingual poet who writes in Hindi, Marathi and English language. She is a writer, author and blogger. Her major themes of poetry are emotions, memories, nature, animal welfare, child welfare and women's welfare.

20. Wisdom

By his solemn steps, I loosen Ethiopian towers,
Amidst high thoughts hidden in my vacant mind,
As the youth emit thru' the volcanic-hours,
On all sides to smear a rapid Rover-frank-kind.

To be shed like inherent inspirations, in times,
And beamy-acquiring-motives to hold his way,
In the two lovely lonesome lips, tasted hymns,
Like the majesty of upper-sphere whom, obey.

See your sport-bent-eyes, only universal abyss,
Where Black-Holes and Aliens, playing eagerly,
With the scale-measured-slacking-dreams lies,
Portal flowed the organ of Greece's wisdom solely.

At length two eyes on the lone Sicilian shower,
Restrain your morning-dawned dynamic power.

© Krishnasankar Acharjee

Krishnasankar Acharjee (Kolkata, West Bengal, India)

krishnasankar.acharjee1122@gmail.com

He is an international freelance writer, poet and author with several Global Awards such as the Gold Pen, Gold Medal, Benjamin Award, and the King of the Letters from Cuba-America. He is an English teacher and Selected two Honorable Doctorates from National University in the USA and Commonwealth Vocational University in the UK.

21. Whom Shall I compare ?

Whom shall I compare you, Mother?
To Earth, to Sky, the Ocean or to God?
Who equals you in the whole world?
Is there anyone who can surpass her kind?

Can one find her in the entire land?
To the earth! Nay, you are still more tolerant,
To the Sky! Nay, your heart is more Vast,
To the Ocean! Nay, your Love is deeper.

To the God! Hardly, because you are ever Near,
To care, to love, to guide, and to inspire,
Filial fear and griefs anon away you chased,
Day and night with Kangaroo's love you nursed.

Her role in my life is always like a lodestar,
Boasts of my life's bounties ever,
Thee I owe,
With reverential gratitude, at Thy feet I bow.

*© **Krishna Walikar.***

Krishna Walikar (Gokak, Karnataka, India)

krishnawalikar55@gmail.com

He began his literary Journey eight years back and his main hobby is literature and music. He wrote many poems in Kannada and English. He won several awards in poetry. He is President, Admin, moderator and Group expert in international poetry groups. He is B.A. and a retired Administrative Officer of the Education department of the Government of Karnataka.

22. Nurturer Always

From a creator to a nurturer,
From deep securities, to love.

From infinite Hope to beliefs,
From refined protection to safekeeping.

From meaningful advice to warnings,
From nesting to freedom.

From intense care to nourishment,
From wanting to hold on, to let go.

O' Mother, the abode of tranquil peace and unconditional support,
You! a humble woman, have been there.

To protect and provide for every life that lives,
In our hearts, you always exist.

©? Lakshmi Ajoy

Lakshmi Ajoy (Mumbai, Maharashtra, India)

ashwini04182@gmail.com

She is a spiritual healer, writer, artist, photographer, solo traveller, adventure sports enthusiast, mountaineer, entrepreneur and social worker. She is a member of various poetry groups on Facebook and has won several awards. Her aim is to spread happiness and joy all around and help others realize the value and essence of life. Writing helps her to give wings to her imagination and live her dreams.

23. Women Are Special

The woman is great for me,
It's the meaning of life,
Faith in oneself,
I give love to everyone,
Women are special.

Women are great,
Because without them,
I would be dead,
So, I say,
Women are special.

Because I give my word,
Respect and peace,
Happiness and joy,
Women are great,
Women are special.

© Maid Corbic

Maid Corbic (Bosnia and Herzegovina)

detrix233@gmail.com

He is a young writer who is passionate about poetry. He also selflessly helps others around him. He is the moderator of the World Literature Forum 'World Literature Forum Peace and Humanity' in Bhutan. He is also the editor of the First Virtual Art portalled by Dijana Uherek Stevanovic and the selector of the competition on a page of the same name that aims to bring together all poets around the world his face. He is a diploma holder in Graphics and Web design.

24. Courage

The woman is beautiful, a woman is charming,
Her body is well-shaped, has sharp meanders,
Her presence has a unique aromatic aroma,
She is the creator and shows light to the world.

Brings colors of jollity, to brighten the world,
She is soft-hearted, patient yet fearless,
She is unstoppable if determined,
Can touch the limit, the sky, the Moon.

She is fragile, but not "delicate darling" only,
Moves forward with confident steps, when required,
Capable of filling the world with happiness,
Received failures too, but not disheartened.

She was considered the "weaker sex" always,
So ironical, she has been entrusted with the toughest tasks,
Which she does with wholeheartedness,
YES, feels proud that I'm a woman.

© Manjula Asthana Mahanti

Manjula Asthana Mahanti

(Bhubaneswar, Odisha, India)
manju.a.mahanti@gmail.com

She is a trilingual poet, author, editor, translator and storyteller. She has got eight collections of books, and her writings are a part of National, and International anthologies, e-magazines, etc. She is the recipient of several awards from Gujarat and Telangana Sahitya Academy along with the "Icons of Asia " Award recently. She is a postgraduate in Sociology and Hindi, Graduatte in English, Honors, Sangeet Prabhakar (vocal) and B. Ed. She worked in college as Senior Lecturer, and last as a High school Principal.

25. Sings Through Life

A mother sings through life,
To support every steep road,
So as not to fall covered in sorrow,
A happy radiated even though the sadness hit.

Your love is like a smooth dew,
Your conscience is biased,
Calm struggling facing lunge,
So that the buds of love are joyful.

For all kinds of challenges,
Faith is always strong
Intentions are strong and firm,
Prioritize dedication, not achievement.

Real love for family and motherland,
The precipitate of a dedication,
Is the sun behind the clouds,
End of a fight for children's happiness.

© *Mário de Oliveira Pires*

Mário de Oliveira Pires (Dilli, Timor Leste)

marioolive34@gmail.com

He is a poet, author, writer and translator. He is a member of several poetry groups on Facebook and has won many awards in poetry contests. His poems are placed in several anthologies, magazines, and newspapers. He has worked as a translator in the Communications Department of the Dili Archdiocese.

26. Devi

You call me Devi,
As I am in a feminine body,
You invoke me with all, your affluence,
Seeking blessings with obeisance.

Yet, You are biased, toward your daughter,
Towards your beloved, towards your mother,
For you, menstruation is taboo,
The daughter is a burden too.

Why treat them as untouchable to their inner sanctum?
To the ordinary woman, why set an ultimatum?
Like me, all women are in a feminine body,
Then why difference and hypocrisy?

Expecting dividends, you all worship me,
Just because I am a Devi,
What is in a body, dear world?
Why forget that first, we are all pristine souls?

*© **Mousumee Baruah***

Mousumee Baruah (Gurgaon, Haryana, India)

mousumimamu@rediffmail.com

She is a bi-lingual freelance writer and poet. Many of her poems and short stories are published in various National & International literary platforms, anthologies, blogzines, etc. She has won several awards in her literary journey. She is the author of the poetry collection, "The Castaway". She is a Master's in English. She worked as a lecturer.

27. Weak but Not Meek

Weak but not meek,
I have a voice,
Though I don't have a choice
I am the maker of a home.

But is there a place I can call home,
I am alone in the streets,
The land is no Persian rug for my feet,
I am ogled at by strangers.

If my walk dares show its independence,
What place is this where I can't lift,
The soaring calls of my soul,
What people are these who want to gobble.

The success of my dreams,
I visualize my mother's face,
Mixed emotions of joy and pain,
When I was pulled out of her womb.

© Nosheen Irfan

Nosheen Irfan (Lahore, Punjab, Pakistan)

noshy.qureshi194@gmail.com

She is a poet by heart. She has contributed to various International poetry anthologies on topics of great relevance to the current times. She holds a master's degree in English Literature and is a teacher by profession.

28. My Reflection

My reflection in the mirror gazing back at me,
Reveals that I have nothing but fear for me,
For I carry the legacy of womankind,
Tales of agonies against our bodies and mind.

The roar inside me is an accumulation,
Of tears, pain, and humiliation,
Hold my hand and feel this tremble away,
I know being strong takes practice every day.

But there's no burden, my soul cannot bear,
I can let the mirror go, fall and shatter,
I'll take the dare and be the woman I want to be,
I'll be brave enough to fight my battle bravely.

I dare to remove all obstacles,
And can rewrite my story with all possibles,
I'm the shaper of my own life,
Will sow the seed of love yet again to thrive.

© Pragyan Parimita Nanda

Pragyan Parimita Nanda (Guwahati, Assam, India)

m123.nanda@gmail.com

She is a trilingual creative writer in Odia, Hindi and English languages. She writes in different journals both Print and magazines, plus on online platforms Instagram and Facebook. She is a homemaker, a trained journalist, a voracious reader, and a passionate writer who loves to travel and explore new places. She is M. A in Journalism.

29. A Woman of Earth

I am strong, I am invincible, I am a woman,
Nothing is impossible for a determined woman.
Little girls with dreams become women with vision,
I am just a good woman with some bad habits.

I speak so much better when I am silent,
I was quiet, but I was not blind.
A woman should have two things,
Who and what she wants.

Women are the real architects of society,
Strong women don't have attitudes.
If you want something to do, ask a woman,
As a woman l can say we are more mature than a man.

As a woman l want to fight against girl's foeticide.
The most adorable thing a woman can have is confidence.
Women are the most beautiful creatures in the world.
From top to bottom of society, women are the leaders.

© Dr. Prasanna Kumar Mohapatra

Dr. Prasanna Kumar Mohapatra (Odisha, Bhubaneshwar, India)

pkmo.kbl@gmail.com

He is a budding writer who started his poetic journey 1 year ago. He is a member of various poetry groups on Facebook and has achieved a lot of recognition for his poetry. He is a founder of a poetry group, 'United Poets@ Heart'. He is encouraging many poets through his group. He is post graduate of and M.Sc in Applied Mathematics. He is retired from LnT company in Odisha and working in LIC company at present.

30. I Shall Perhaps Ask

The morning beckons with the wonder of costume,
The sun is like a mirror fresh and clean to reflect,
Flowers colored their lips from the rays of the sun,
Women gleamed with tattooed faces from hills,
Hairpins in plaited hair and nose ring sparkle.

Who will buy it ? A nude child beside the parrots
Cautiously looks at people circumspectly busy,
Trapped in so many questions about shifting home,
Shifting mother ever dear to children for love,
If sold who will understand those hot tears.

Eventually, a man agrees in bargains,
In obeisance to her milk, she stands mute,
Drops of tears she takes as money,
I was frozen even on a sweaty summer day,
The morning was snapped out from the sky.

©Rajendra K. Padhi

Rajendra K Padhi (Bhubaneswar, Odisha, India)

rajendrapadhi62@gmail.com

He is a poet, Novelist, Editor and Translator. He has translated many stories, biographies and poems from Odia into English. He has written 5 books including poetry and novels. His articles, poems,and interviews are published in more than 80 books, and journals from different countries of the world. He has been a keynote speaker address in both National and International conferences. He a retired professor in English.

31. Gifted by God

Everyone must have one,
They care like none,
All they need is security,
Love and more safety.

Girl child is gifted by God,
And can easily be termed as demigod,
Their love is unconditional,
Their importance is phenomenal.

We have to respect every girl child,
And must nurture them to be bold,
They fill the universe with garlands of love,
For divine reason they sent from above.

Everyone has to give them strength to succeed,
Because, Nation's growth depends on them indeed,
In every aspect give them confidence,
The results will be different with their presence.

© Rajesh Sharma Brahmabhatla

Rajesh Sharma (Khammam, Telangana, India)

rajeshpa09@gmail.com

He is a bilingual poet. He writes in English and Telugu languages. He is an Admin of various poetry groups on Facebook. He has authored one English poetry book 'Hey Honey'. His writings are the part of several anthologies, newspapers and magazines. He has received many awards for his poetry. He is BSc in Computer Science and presently works for the Government of his state in the Panchaytraj Dept.

32. Female (Fe(Iron)+male)

Power is the name of a woman,
A perfect example of balance and patience,
You are female Fe(Iron)+male,
Strong like iron added in the life of a male.

You can live and cherish the moment,
You are allowed to take a walk on the wild side,
And to escape into that crazy, fun side of yourself,
You can decide to live a gamble, or to live a better life,
You can tackle mourning and grief.

But don't forget,
You are also a human,
You are not allowed to be vulnerable,
And to have space to do things that bring joy,
A bird without wings an enchantress, a thunderstorm in the skin,
You are amazing in every form.

© Ranjana Kashyap

Ranjana Kashyap (Jhakri, Himachal Pradesh, India)

ranj77in23@gmail.com

She is a poet, writer and artist. She is a member of various poetry groups on social media. She has contributed her poems to several anthologies, magazines, newspapers and blogs. Her paintings have been placed on various literary platforms. She is a passionate lover of nature. She holds the degree of M.A., B. Ed, ADCA and Art History.

33. Eight Long Winters

Eight winters I am without her touch,
Time flies fast,
Still, her beauty haunts me,
Her smile I perceive.

As she appears before my vision,
This mundane existence then transforms to a joyful life,
I shake myself off to reach my mission,
In the realms of effusive poems, where this heart lies.

Time fly,
Maa remains constant in my life,
With the wish of the Providence, she crossed the bar,
Leaving behind all the cares at bay.

Now, as my hairs turn all grey.
Revive our moments to cast my worries afar,
And Eight long Winters I am without any sort of fear,
I smile, not shedding a single drop of a tear.

© Rimni Chakravarty

Rimni Chakravarty (Siliguri, West Bengal, India)

rimnichakravarty@gmail.com

She is passionate about poetry, music, art and literature. She has got more than 50 publications, 6 book chapters, and two best paper presentation awards in quest of reaching a platform in the world of literature. She is M.A.(English), B.ED, Asst. Professor, and Humanities.

34. I Lose My Way

Attired in the gown of gaiety,
Sowing seeds of cheerful chrysanthemum,
Flying on the flag of fortitude,
I took the road to dell.

Harmonious hues of nature beckoned me,
Titanic- tall trees embraced me in glee,
In the solitude of wondrous woods,
I treaded on the untrodden path.

An expedition to the unknown and unseen,
Light and dark, net of air and alternate,
Endeavouring to take directions,
In the vacant wilderness.

Destinations are hard to find,
It turns out to be a journey to the interior of the mind,
I lose my way,
To find Thee "O my Lord" in life's sway.

© Ritu Kamra Kumar

Dr Ritu Kamra Kumar (Yamunanagar, Haryana, India)

ritukumar.gmn@gmail.com

She is an avid writer, poet and academic. She has contributed more than 350 write-ups, articles and poems in several National newspapers and magazines, and many research papers in National and International research journals and anthologies. She is the Editor in Chief of her College Magazine. She has authored three books. She is M., M. Phil, and Ph.D. in English Literature, and working as a HOD and Associate Professor in the Post Graduate Department of English.

35. She

She fills the room with her chuckles and chortles,
Creating a symphony delightfully aural,
She is a daughter, she is a woman.

She is as beautiful as the dance of a peacock
She is as gentle as the feather of a white dove,
She is grace, she is a woman.

She is the epitome of love and devotion,
She can get her husband back from the god of death,
She is a wife, she is a woman.

She is at times as silent as a night,
Or is a furious storm, do not dare her might,
She has fortitude, she is a woman.

She is an embodiment of care and compassion,
She nurtures selflessly and with passion,
She is a mother, she is a woman.

© Roopam Chadha

Roopam Chadha(Delhi, India)

harpreetchadha6@gmail.com

She is a bilingual poet. She has authored two books of English poetry. She received an award for her debut anthology and the Canaries Sing On' from 'Autism for Help Village Project'. Her second anthology 'Blushing Candles' has been published recently. Her poems share space in several National and International anthologies. Besides writing, painting is also her passion. She is a graduate of Economics.

36. O' My Gardenia

O' what was it, wafting on wings of a breeze,
Whispering through my windows ajar?
While I was waiting for a lone traveller,
Who promised to sit for a minute by my bed.

With a bowl of gardenia that,
My senses waited for,
Floating on a puddle my tears had made,
Or was it buried musk you wore on your flesh.

Dancing in the boughs as you ride your way,
You stalked my fields alone hunting,
My senses in the dying crimson of a sunset,
Yes I know, you tried to send me.

New sheaves of corn that touched your soil,
And a fallen flower by the road, you picked,
And what did I send? Just the worn-out gardenia,
That still sent a whiff of a lost teardrop.

© Saheli Mitra

Saheli Mitra (Kolkata, West Bengal, India)

moonchitu15@gmail.com

She is a social entrepreneur, journalist, author and poet, who runs her own content and creative company, 'Tales Talks & Walks' with an experience of 25 years as a Journalist. She has got more than 200 published articles to her credit. She is an author of the Internationally launched romantic thriller 'Lost Words' and a co-author of several short story collections and poetry anthologies. She is M. Phil in Environmental Biology.

37. Pseudo Family Honour

Being born as a girl baby I am called sister,
Alike brother I have got nurtured well by my mother,
Gifts have been different from him on my cradle ceremony,
Toy babies, toy utensils, and the clothing of babies are seen presented.

So forth, games are restricted not allowed to play marbles,
Since age seven sweeping has been an obligatory duty,
I wish the same should have been asked him as well,
He is free to meet and play with peers.

While I will be confined to my house owing to gender bias,
My ability of employability is encouraged not enough,
My sincere service to the family is recognized not,
My pursuit of personal growth is valued not.

Alike brother I too possess dreams and wishes as such,
But of pseudo Family- Honour he is attributed with,
Alas! All of mine, where I am born,
Have been sold out in the custom called marriage.

© Sane Shiva Shanker

Sane Shiva Shanker (Mahabubnagar, Telangana, India)

saneshivashanker@gmail.com

He is a poet and writer. He is a member of various poetry groups on social media. He has contributed many poems to several anthologies, magazines, newspapers, and blogs. By profession, he is a senior teacher in English.

38. Temple of Worship

Replete with emotions,
A synonym of patience, O' woman,
You are a quintessence.

An enamoured soul, kind, mellow, and pure,
the mother of mankind; a fragrant flower,
a serene stream; an entity, unique.

Inner strength, replete within your silhouette,
the whole cosmos sleeps,
You are a shelter, in thy bosom love is conceived.

Grown and nourished, you are a saviour,
Oblivious of other's flaws, a forgiver always,
Brings forth the best in others, you're a selfless creature.

O' woman, you are a temple of worship, so sacred,
A being to be loved and adored,
An impeccable personage.

© Seema Sharma

Seema Sharma (Delhi, India)

seemashar0807@gmail.com

She is a poet, writer and author. She is passionate about nature and reading books. She is a peace lover and believes in providing new horizons to her life. She is an active member of several literary platforms and participates in various literary activities. Her poems are part of several magazines, anthologies, and newspapers. She is a teacher by profession with MA in English.

39. Amalgamation

The embodiment of beauty and looks,
Provoke desire to love and being loved,
Surrenders herself like a flowing brook.

Draped with dreams and so perfectly curved,
Sets up the fire with passion and fervor,
Hosting with flamboyance, only a few are served.

Seems like a work of art by a skilled carver,
With the hues of rainbows and butterflies,
Distinguished as subtle wood smoke savour.

The aura begins where ecstasy lies,
Life is a game of severe emotions,
People in self-love seldom find allies.

Love develops a bond with absorption,
A woman is an ocean of love,
Making even an ordinary place heaven.

*© **Shafia Afzal***

Shafia Afzal (Islamabad, Punjab, Pakistan)

afzalshafia5@gmail.com

She is a bilingual writer and poet. She writes in English and Urdu language. Reading and writing have been her passion since childhood. She is a member of several renowned literary forums on Social media. Her articles have been published in various National newspapers. She holds a degree of B.SC, in Statistics, Mathematics, and Economics.

40. Believe or Not

I am born free, I want to be free,
Freedom of expression,
My profession is very dear to me.

I believe in toto,
The beliefs of my mother
Have guided me to Suo Moto.

I will live up to the mark, I believe so,
Genetically, physically,
I may not be strong,
But, in my attitude,
Outlook, I am headstrong.

The autobiographies guide me,
The situations daily, Test me,
I believe and keep building my potential,
I will face the challenges, in life, and fight too.

© Shelleyandra Kapil

Shelleyandra Kapil (Chandigarh, India)

kapilirts@gmail.com

He is a poet, reviewer and writer. He writes in Hindi, Punjabi and English languages. He has authored 6 books. His poems are published in various literary magazines, books, newspapers and anthologies. He has achieved several awards in his professional as well as literary fields. He is M.A in Public Administration. He has retired as Principal Chief Commercial Manager from North Central Railways, Priyagraj.

41. Gandhari

Because I am a woman,
I had to put a man's blindness in my eyes,
And hide their spark inside the blindfold,
To smother the voice of protest under it.

To stand by a man obsessed with,
Blind love for the scepter,
I saw and did not see at the same time,
A woman's modesty outraged.

In the royal court of hypocrisy,
I could not stop the act but stopped the,
Curse that disrobed dignity,
Flicked at the bold, brazen heroes.

And because I am a woman,
I used the fire in my eyes to protect myself.
The evil born off me but hoped,
That in the end truth would triumph.

© Dr. Snehaprava Das

Dr. Snehaprava Das (Bhubaneswar, Odisha, India)

dassnehaprava@gmail.com

She is an eminent poet and translator. She has translated several Odia fictions, nonfictions, plays and poems into English. She has five collections of English. She has received the Prabashi Bhasha Sahitya Samman, the Fakirmohan Anubad Samman, and the Jibanananda Das award for her translations. She is M.A, and Ph. D in English.

42. I Am Here

The playground was slippery
and they returned with mud
on dresses.

Ma, we couldn't play in
stipulated time, as the place
was not pretty well.

Don't be panic dears,
it will be clear within a
couple of days.

Come to the dining table,
I have a special dish for you,
Saying this, she rushed
to the oven, and baked
something new.

Their faces turned bright
as the burner when started
Love of a mother they perceived.

© Sreedharan Parokode

Sreedharan Parokode (Kozhikode, Kerala, India)

sreeparokode@gmail.com

He is a bilingual poet and lyricist. He writes in English and Malayalam languages. He has thirty books of poems to his credit and has written songs for animation films also. His poems have been well received in different platforms and discussed. He presented his poems in various National and International platforms. He has received several awards and recognitions for his poetry. He beholds the degree of MA (Eco) M.A (Eng), M.A.(Popn Studies) M Phil and a Post Graduate Diploma in Parental Education. He is retired from Calicut University.

43. An Embodiment of Love

She planted a seed of love in her heart,
When she was just ten and two,
She watered it daily without restraint,
And in no time, it unabashedly grew.

Into an all-encompassing tree,
With myriad flowers and leaves new.
None ever met sadness, knew any gloom,
For the love tree in her was in full bloom.

An angel then struck a heavenly arrow,
That caused a few flowers to fall.
Love bled unwittingly from her good heart,
She poured it out freely, not for one but all.

A fair lady with an evergreen heart,
She was thus, endearingly looked upon.
With age which never became barren,
And flowers and fruits of love grew on and on.

© Srividya Subramanian

Srividya Subramanian (Chennai, Tamil Nadu, India)

srivi1971@gmail.com

She is a poet, writer, and author. She writes poetry, stories, articles and essays. She is an active member of several literary platforms on social media. Her poems are part of several magazines, anthologies, and newspapers. Her other hobbies include cooking and listening to music. She is a teacher by profession. She has won a lot of recognition for her work.

44. Pinnacle of Beauty

The beauty of a woman is not just the beauty of her face,
But it can be found in her attitude and grace,
It is not always about the dressing style,
It can also be found in her innocent smile.

The soul of her beauty lies in her heart,
Her beauty is within her, and is an art,
She is like a swan whose beauty radiates to the morning sun,
With a sweet smile, that is worth millions.

There is a garden in her face,
Where roses and white lilies blow,
An angel living in a heavenly paradise,
Wherein all the pleasant fruits grow.

She is the queen of her own world,
She is the hope, she is the pinnacle,
She is astonishing, she is wonderful,
She is charming and the most beautiful.

© Dr. Suboohi Jafar

Dr. Suboohi Jafar (Varanasi, UP, India)

suboohijafar@gmail.com

She is a young and dynamic poet, artist and singer by heart, an oncologist by profession. A Soldier in Fight against CANCER. She has won many awards and medals in her academic career. She has received several awards in poetry contests conducted by various poetic groups on Facebook.

45. Substantial Woman

A substantial woman in my life is she,
Not perfect, but obviously the best.
A daughter, sister, wife, and mother,
Totally different from the rest.

Of course, she quarrels with me,
But her heart is very clean.
I know her for more than three decades,
One can understand, really what I mean.

The woman is from Eden: is my abbreviation for WIFE,
So, she cannot be wrong,
Angel of Paradise, and not an ordinary woman,
I have been walking with her for so long.

She wants nothing but love and self-respect,
Instead of her sacrifices for the family,
Quid Pro quo, is the best policy,
For happy and peaceful conjugal life, cheerfully.

© Sudhir Kumar Nanda

Sudhir Kumar Nanda (Calicut, Kerala, India)

sknanda205@gmail.com

He is a bilingual poet, writer, and author. He writes articles, short stories and quotes. He has published a poetry book entitled 'psalms of Life' and a novel entitled 'Fatal adolescence'. He has achieved several awards in literary contests. He is an active member of various poetry groups on Facebook. He holds a master's degree in Economics and Psychology and Diploma in Creative Writing in English.

46. I Can Hear

I can hear the tune of silence,
All alone in deep resilience.

I seek to rise above the bar,
I can see the crowd from afar.

I ponder about the folks,
They satire me behind my back.

It's all because I try to resist,
Still, with me, my fights will persist.

I am a woman of an elegant kind,
And I will choose to stride.

They query about my mystery,
Let them design a dirty story.

I have chosen to foster my spirit,
Like a rising star, I'll adorn the nights.

© Sudipta Mishra

Sudipta Mishra (Bhubaneshwar, Odisha, India)

sudiptamishra71@gmail.com

She is a multi-faceted artist and dancer excelling in various fields of art and culture. She has weaved more than a hundred books. Her book, 'The Essence of Life', is credited with Amazon bestseller, and 'The Songs of My Heart' is scaling newer heights of glory. She has garnered numerous accolades in literature, including the famous Rabindranath Tagore Memorial. She regularly pens articles in newspapers as a strong female voice. She is a research scholar, perusing a Ph.D. in English.

47. Dynamic Woman

Breaking out of a nutshell,
From darkness to light,
Dynamic personalities pave the way,
To showcase their hidden talents.

Not only with the cutlery in the kitchen,
In all fields, shining out,
A visionary who foresees the future.
Fighting for the injustices seen.

A tree that stands on its own,
From Jhansi Rani to Droupadi Murmu,
A role model in shaping society,
Each and every woman is unique.

Toughness, stoic the attributes,
My own observation and feelings,
Proud to see women working hard for survival,
Rising up, like waves from the sea.

*© **Sulochna Narayanan***

Sulochana Narayanan (Palakkad, Kerala, India)

sulsubra@gmail.com

She is a lover of arts like paintings, music and poetry. She has recently published her first book "Imprints: An Anthology of Poems". She is a member of various poetry groups on Facebook and has won several awards. She is M.A English and has done B.Ed. She is an academician by profession for the past 11 years.

48. Divine Power

A woman I'm, belong to the divine power,
Within every woman has the shower of a warrior,
As a daughter, wife, mother, and mother-in-law,
I treat a home with my unconditional shines,
And give birth to a world from my unselfish womb.

A woman I'm, a symbol of voice,
Against injustices, harassment, and violence,
With the right of dignity, I can defeat all enemies
Because in every step of adversities,
I can show the pristine powers of Maa Durga.

I'm the altar of hymns,
The temple of peace,
Without reciprocal, I give and give the world,
As I am blessed with,
A divine power.

© Sumi Kapaheru

Sumi Kapahera (Morigaon, Assam, India)

debend557@gmail.com

She is a poet by passion. At present, she is involved with many wonderful poetry platforms and literary organizations. She has achieved many awards including Gujarat Sahitya Academy certificates. She is an M.A. in English and BED, a teacher by profession.

49. She Is Unique

The unique membrane and the finest string in her,
Waiting for the eagerness of some renowned Maestro,
They demand the intimate touch of an efficient finger.
But sounds out of tune if hammered with a sudden blow.

She is the woman; the most sophisticated thing of creation,
And everything beautiful has been created for her.
She can beautify the ugliest by her glance and by her passion,
As the darkest sky can be beautified by one dazzling star.

Her action form the opposite side can change the inertial state,
Of the most inactive person found on the earth.
Her blessing hands can change the effects of ill fate,
And her presence brings happiness in home and heart.

© Swapan Kumar Rakshit

Swapan Kumar Rakshit (Bankura, West Bengal, India)

rakshit.swapan2015@gmail.com

He is a poet and writer. His major genera of poetry is composing sonnets. He is a member of various literary groups on Facebook and actively participates in several contests. He has received many prizes for his poetry. His writings are the part of many newspapers, magazines and anthologies. He wants to be acquainted with the universal passionate minds of the poets. By profession, he is a Physics teacher.

50. An Abuse

A girl child is not a boon or adorning gift,
A male child is a bliss without resentment or rift.

A girl is assessed as a financial burden and drift,
Social perceptions and perspectives are so clift.

To eliminate this difference between a son and daughter is not swift,
Education stamped as authoritative to the 'son' considered as fit.

Girls are compelled to stay, without education in their cockpit,
Toiling hard in the house hold work they are mere puppets.

Priorities to the male child are preferential of their fulfilment,
The girl's desires are caged in her mind for want of procurement.

The city scenario is a bit changing but without progress or upliftment,
Rays of hope are dim but there is a chance of betterment.

© **Uma Natrajan**

Uma Natarajan (Ratlam, MP, India)

uma1948@yahoo.com

She is an artist who uses words as her medium, She has published 15 books of poetry in English and 2 books of Hindi poetry. She has contributed various articles in various books in English and Hindi. Her dream is to continue writing and contributing to the field of literature. She actively participates in various literary contests and has won several awards. She holds masters in English and has served as an English teacher for many years.

(Paperback, 1ˢᵗ Edition, @ January 2023)

Compiled & Edited By: Dr. Sonia Gupta